# Wo

by Gabriel Jordan

HOUGHTON MIFFLIN HARCOURT

ILLUSTRATION CREDIT: 4 Scott MacNeill.

PHOTOGRAPHY CREDITS: Cover ©Steve Maslowski/Photo Researchers, Inc.; 1 ©Mark Bowler/Photo Researchers, Inc.; 2 ©Nigel Cattlin/Photo Researchers, Inc.; 3 ©Mark Bowler/Photo Researchers, Inc.; 6 ©Gari Wyn Williams/Alamy; 7 ©Connie Coleman/Getty Images; 7 ©HMH; 8 ©Getty Images; 9 ©Tierbild Okapia/Photo Researchers, Inc.; 10 ©Corbis.



Printed in China

ISBN: 978-0-547-89073-9

5 6 7 8 9 10 0940 21 20 19 18 17 16 15 14 13

4500416855 A B C D E F G

Are you ready to learn about a special worm? It is called an earthworm.

There are many kinds of earthworms. They do not have legs or eyes.

A worm can move
like a snake.
That means a worm
does not need legs!

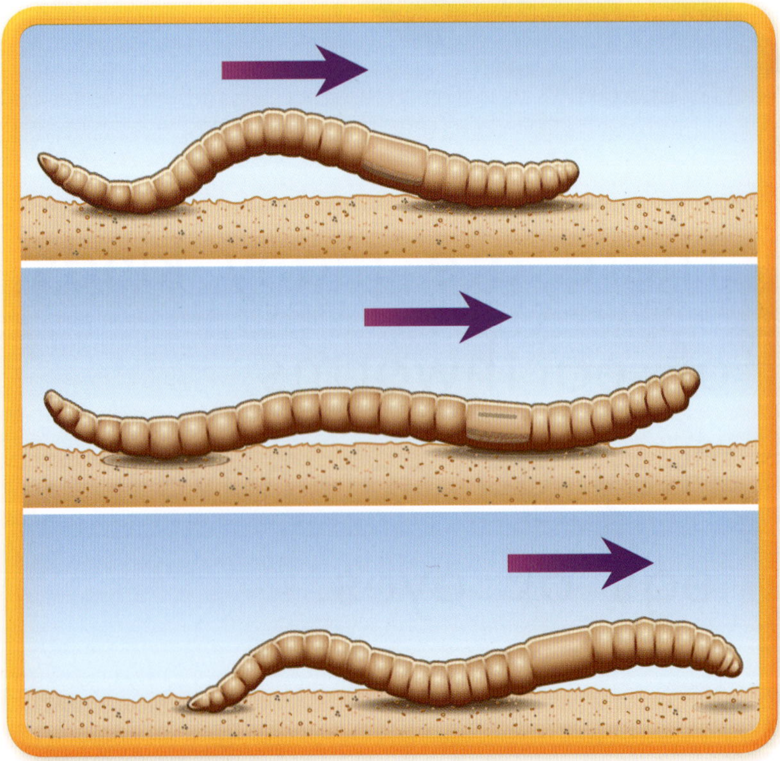

An earthworm usually lives under the earth. It is too dark to see, so a worm does not need eyes.

When it rains, the soil
gets wet.
Then a worm might
come above the ground.

When it rains, you can find many worms on the ground.
You can find them in the country or the city.

What if you step on
a worm?
Do not feel too bad.
A worm can grow parts
back again!

When the rain stops,
the sun warms the earth.
Then the worm
goes back under the soil.

A worm makes a trail of sticky slime. The slime covers almost everything. That is why a worm feels slimy when you pick it up.

# Responding

## WORDS TO KNOW Word Builder

What is one kind of worm?

## Talk About It

**Text to World** Have you ever seen an earthworm? Where did you see it?

## WORDS TO KNOW

| | |
|---|---|
| almost | kinds |
| country | ready |
| covers | soil |
| earth | warms |

## TARGET STRATEGY Question

Ask questions about what you are reading.